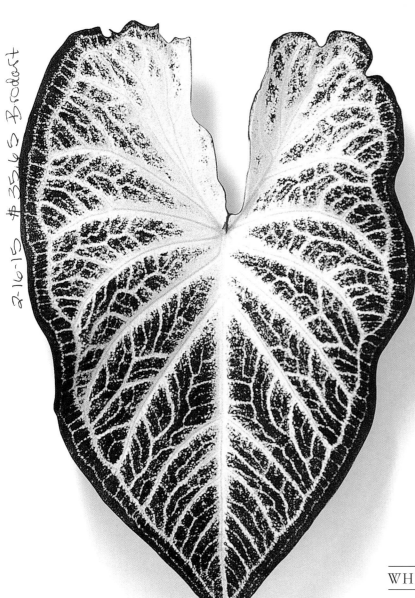

WHEN I READ THE BOOK

When I read the book, the biography famous,
And is this then (said I) what the author calls a man's life?
And so will someone when I am dead and gone write my life?
(As if any man really knew aught of my life,
Why even I myself I often think know little or nothing of my real life,
Only a few hints, a few diffused faint clews and indirections
I seek for my own use to trace out here.)

From "Inscriptions," *Leaves of Grass*

· V O I C E S ·
· I N   P O E T R Y ·

WALT WHITMAN NANCY LOEWEN

ILLUSTRATIONS BY ROB DAY

CREATIVE EDUCATION

"Do I contradict myself? Very well, then I contradict myself, I am large, I contain multitudes"—words, curious words, written by the son of a Brooklyn carpenter. Walt Whitman (1819–92) spent only five years in school. But reading, teaching, practicing journalism, and mingling with the masses left him with a profound idea: Poetry must break away from the old European pattern, identified by strict, staid adherence to rhyme and to metrical forms and a much-too-confining notion of "place."

Embracing the Emersonian view that "America is a poem in our eyes," Whitman believed that "the United States themselves are essentially the greatest poem." He scoffed at verse distilled from other verse, rejected fiction and romance in favor of what was truly genuine, and sought to discover in the common man and woman the temper and toil of their lives.

In 1854, Whitman returned to his parents' home to write his masterpiece, *Leaves of Grass*. Incorporating new poems into later versions of the book, he struggled most of his life to make the public appreciate its virtues. His poetry eschewed high-flown language for unglamorous, everyday speech and colloquialisms. The book's emotional intensity and intuitive power were completely radical at the time of its appearance. Ralph Waldo Emerson hailed the book as "the most extraordinary piece of wit and wisdom that America has yet contributed."

Walt Whitman was the first poet to write extensively in free verse, but his critics outnumbered the early admirers of his liberating lines. Scandalized by the poet's sexual frankness, some called him amoral, egotistical, Bohemian, anti-intellectual, or simply infantile in his celebration of the human body. His attackers considered his poetry formless and distasteful.

Perhaps it is enough to say that our preeminent American poet was far ahead of his time, for what was revolutionary to readers yesterday seems commonplace today.

As Ezra Pound once said of Whitman, "He is America."

— *J. Patrick Lewis, United States Children's Poet Laureate (2011-13)*

"It is I you hold and who holds you. I spring from the pages into your arms," wrote Walt Whitman in *Leaves of Grass*, a collection of poetry that is regarded as one of the world's literary masterpieces.

In his poems and in his life, Whitman celebrated the human spirit and the human body; he sang the praises of democracy and chronicled the marvel of technological progress. His direct, speech-like writing style and his frank celebration of sensuality shocked many of his contemporaries. But Whitman persisted despite the criticism his unorthodox work received. He spent more than three decades writing, revising, and expanding *Leaves of Grass*, and his influence on the development of modern American poetry has been both profound and enduring.

Walt Whitman

SONG OF MYSELF

Section 1

I celebrate myself, and sing myself,
And what I assume you shall assume,
For every atom belonging to me as good belongs to you.

I loafe and invite my soul,
I lean and loafe at my ease observing a spear of summer grass.

My tongue, every atom of my blood, form'd from this soil,
      this air,
Born here of parents born here from parents the same, and
      their parents the same,
I, now thirty-seven years old in perfect health begin,
Hoping to cease not till death.

Creeds and schools in abeyance,
Retiring back a while sufficed at what they are, but
      never forgotten,
I harbor for good or bad, I permit to speak at every hazard,
Nature without check with original energy.

From "Inscriptions," *Leaves of Grass*

CHILDHOOD

Walt Whitman was born on May 31, 1819, in the rural village of West Hills, Long Island, New York. He was the second child of Walter and Louisa Whitman. Of the nine children born to them, one son died in infancy; one had an intellectual disability; one was insane; one died at a young age of alcoholism and tuberculosis; and, of course, one grew up to join the ranks of the world's greatest poets.

Walt's earliest memories were infused with the salty smell of the sea and the rhythmic pounding of the Atlantic surf. Alone or with friends, he dug for clams, speared eels, explored inlets, rode the ferries, and tagged along with boat pilots and dockhands. When he was four, the family moved to the rapidly expanding city of Brooklyn, where his father worked as a carpenter. The Whitmans returned to Long Island often, however, and both settings were explored in the poet's work.

Walt Whitman's birthplace, Long Island, New York

THERE WAS A CHILD WENT FORTH

There was a child went forth every day,
And the first object he look'd upon, that object
      he became,
And that object became part of him for the day
      or a certain part of the day,
Or for many years or stretching cycles of years.

The early lilacs became part of this child,
And grass and white and red morning-glories,
      and white and red clover, and the song
      of the phoebe-bird,
And the Third-month lambs and the sow's pink-faint
      litter, and the mare's foal and the cow's calf,
And the noisy brood of the barnyard or by the mire of
      the pond-side,
And the fish suspending themselves so curiously below
      there, and the beautiful curious liquid,
And the water-plants with their graceful flat heads, all
      became part of him.

The field-sprouts of Fourth-month and Fifth-month
      became part of him,
Winter-grain sprouts and those of the light-yellow
      corn, and the esculent roots of the garden,

(continued)

9

And the apple-trees cover'd with blossoms and the fruit afterward, and
        wood-berries, and the commonest weeds by the road,
And the old drunkard staggering home from the outhouse of the tavern
        whence he had lately risen,
And the schoolmistress that pass'd on her way to the school,
And the friendly boys that pass'd, and the quarrelsome boys,
And the tidy and fresh-cheek'd girls, and the barefoot negro boy and girl,
And all the changes of city and country wherever he went.

His own parents, he that had father'd him and she that had conceiv'd
        him in her womb and birth'd him,
They gave this child more of themselves than that,
They gave him afterward every day,
        they became part of him.

The mother at home quietly placing the dishes
        on the supper-table,
The mother with mild words, clean her cap and gown, a wholesome
        odor falling off her person and clothes as she walks by,
The father, strong, self-sufficient, manly, mean, anger'd, unjust,
The blow, the quick loud word, the tight bargain, the crafty lure,
The family usages, the language, the company, the furniture, the yearning
        and swelling heart,
Affection that will not be gainsay'd, the sense of what is real, the thought
        if after all it should prove unreal,

The doubts of day-time and the doubts of night-time, the
    curious whether and how,
Whether that which appears so is so, or is it all flashes and
    specks?
Men and women crowding fast in the streets, if they are not
    flashes and specks what are they?
The streets themselves and the façades of houses, and goods
    in the windows,
Vehicles, teams, the heavy-plank'd wharves, the huge crossing
    at the ferries,
The village on the highland seen from afar at sunset, the
    river between,
Shadows, aureola and mist, the light falling on roofs and
    gables of white or brown two miles off,
The schooner near by sleepily dropping down the tide, the
    little boat slack-tow'd astern,
The hurrying tumbling waves, quick-broken crests, slapping,
The strata of color'd clouds, the long bar of maroon-tint
    away solitary by itself, the spread of purity it lies
    motionless in,
The horizon's edge, the flying sea-crow, the fragrance of salt
    marsh and shore mud,
These became part of that child who went forth every day,
    and who now goes, and will always go forth every day.

From "Autumn Rivulets," *Leaves of Grass*

EDUCATION

Walt attended public schools in Brooklyn, where his teachers labeled him "a dreamy and impractical youth." At age 11, he left school and began working as an office boy at a small law firm. One of the lawyers, Walt remembered gratefully, "help'd me at my handwriting and composition, and, (the signal event of my life up to that time,) subscribed for me to a big circulating library." Walt became an avid reader and would remain so the rest of his life.

At age 12, Walt began a printing apprenticeship at a New York newspaper. Like Benjamin Franklin and Mark Twain, Walt received much of his education standing before a hand press, setting lines of type letter by letter. Sometimes he contributed short items to the paper. These small successes so bolstered his courage that he submitted an anonymous article to the *New York Mirror*. His hands trembled as he opened the pages containing his work. "How it made my heart double-beat to see my piece on the pretty white paper, in nice type," he later recalled.

Winter in Brooklyn

WHEN I HEARD THE LEARN'D ASTRONOMER

When I heard the learn'd astronomer,
When the proofs, the figures, were ranged in columns before me,
When I was shown the charts and diagrams, to add, divide, and
      measure them,
When I sitting heard the astronomer where he lectured
      with much applause in the lecture-room,
How soon unaccountable I became tired and sick,
Till rising and gliding out I wander'd off by myself,
In the mystical moist night-air, and from time to time,
Look'd up in perfect silence at the stars.

From "By the Roadside," *Leaves of Grass*

SCHOOLMASTER

Walt graduated as a journeyman printer at the age of 16, but he wasn't able to practice his trade right away. In 1835, a fire ravaged New York's publishing district; later that year a second fire destroyed nearly 700 buildings and threw the city into an economic tailspin. Unable to find work, Walt returned to his family, then farming on Long Island. But Walt refused to do farm work, much to his father's angry bewilderment. Instead, he became a schoolteacher, taking on a series of short appointments in one-room country schoolhouses across Long Island.

The curriculum was basic, and Walt was casual about his teaching duties, preferring open discussions and games of Twenty Questions to more disciplined approaches. While the terms were in session he "boarded round," living a few days at his students' homes, often sleeping on straw mattresses in drafty corners. He was lonely much of the time but later came to appreciate this period as "one of my best experiences and deepest lessons in human nature behind the scenes, and in the masses."

New York City ablaze, December 16, 1835

ONE'S-SELF I SING

One's-self I sing, a simple separate person,
Yet utter the word democratic, the word En-Masse.

Of physiology from top to toe I sing,
Not physiognomy alone nor brain alone is worthy for
    the Muse,
      I say the Form complete is worthier far,
The Female equally with the Male I sing.

Of Life immense in passion, pulse, and power,
Cheerful, for freest action form'd under the laws
    divine,
The Modern Man I sing.

From "Inscriptions," *Leaves of Grass*

PUBLISHER

At 19, Walt bought a secondhand press, rented an office above a stable, and started his own weekly newspaper, the *Long Islander*. The paper contained articles reprinted from larger papers, as well as local-interest stories about prize pumpkins, three-legged cows, and the like. Walt delivered the paper himself, riding his white mare, Nina, and visiting with the farm families as he went along. "I never had happier jaunts," he noted.

After a year, however, Walt became restless and sold the paper. For many years after, he bounced from job to job, working for various newspapers as a printer and often as an editor. He did good work but had a reputation for sloth. "There is a man about our office so lazy that it takes two men to open his jaws when he speaks," gibed the management of the *Aurora*, a New York daily. "If you kick him he's too idle to cry, for then he'd have to wipe his eyes. *What* can be done with him?"

Men at work in a print shop

This is what you shall do: Love the earth and sun and the animals, despise riches, give alms to every one that asks, stand up for the stupid and crazy, devote your income and labor to others, hate tyrants, argue not concerning God, have patience and indulgence toward the people, take off your hat to nothing known or unknown or to any man or number of men, go freely with powerful uneducated persons and with the young and with the mothers of families, read these leaves in the open air every season of every year of your life, re-examine all you have been told at school or church or in any book, dismiss whatever insults your own soul, and your very flesh shall be a great poem and have the richest fluency not only in its words but in the silent lines of its lips and face and between the lashes of your eyes and in every motion and joint of your body.

From the preface to the 1855 edition of *Leaves of Grass*

Whitman may have been lackadaisical about his work sometimes, but he still managed to accomplish a great deal. Between newspaper jobs, he published short stories, poems, and essays in popular magazines; he even published a temperance novel, *Franklin Evans*, as an extra edition of a local paper. Above all, he enjoyed the city of New York. Dressed like a dandy with a top hat, cane, and a flower in his lapel, Whitman adopted the air of a gentleman and immersed himself in the city's parks, theaters, music, art, and opera.

Whitman was also an active member of the Democratic Party and once addressed a rally of 15,000 people. Slavery was the burning question of the day and, for a time, split the party into disputing factions. Whitman joined the Free Soil Democrats, who believed that slavery should be prohibited from all annexed territories. But his outspoken beliefs cost him several important editorial positions, and as he entered his 30s he became disillusioned with political parties and with journalism.

New York's Central Park in Whitman's day

*I*t is the fashion among dillettants and fops (perhaps I myself am not guiltless,) to decry the whole formulation of the active politics of America, as beyond redemption, and to be carefully kept away from. See you that you do not fall into this error. America, it may be, is doing very well upon the whole, notwithstanding these antics of the parties and their leaders, these half-brain'd nominees, the many ignorant ballots, and many elected failures and blatherers. It is the dillettants, and all who shirk their duty, who are not doing well. As for you, I advise you to enter more strongly yet into politics. I advise every young man to do so. Always inform yourself; always do the best you can; always vote. Disengage yourself from parties. They have been useful, and to some extent remain so; but the floating, uncommitted electors, farmers, clerks, mechanics, the masters of parties—watching aloof, inclining victory this side or that side—such are the ones most needed, present and future. For America, if eligible at all to downfall and ruin, is eligible within herself, not without; for I see clearly that the combined foreign world could not beat her down. But these savage, wolfish parties alarm me. Owning no law but their own will, more and more combative, less and less tolerant of the idea of ensemble and of equal brotherhood, the perfect equality of the States, the ever-over-arching American ideas, it behooves you to convey yourself implicitly to no party, nor submit blindly to their dictators, but steadily hold yourself judge and master over all of them.

From *Democratic Vistas*

EMERGENCE

Trading in his top hat and cane for laborer's denim and a wide-brimmed hat, Whitman did a little carpentry work with his father and brothers, speculated in real estate, and for a while operated his own print shop. Other young men were heading west, seeking adventure and California gold, but Whitman was content among the myriad faces on the streets of his city. He rode stagecoaches just to talk to the drivers; his friends included mechanics and ferryboat hands. In all his doings, he carried with him a notebook in order to more easily capture his thoughts. Gradually the jottings became more urgent. Wrote biographer Justin Kaplan, "In his green notebook the printer, schoolmaster, fiction writer, editor, shopkeeper, and house builder began—for the first time, as far as anyone knows—to sound his voice over the roofs of the world."

Whitman in 1854

Section 19

This is the meal equally set, this the meat for
    natural hunger,
It is for the wicked just the same as the righteous,
    I make appointments with all,
I will not have a single person slighted or left away,
The kept-woman, sponger, thief, are hereby invited,
The heavy-lipp'd slave is invited, the venerealee is invited;
There shall be no difference between them and the rest.

This is the press of a bashful hand, this the float and
    odor of hair,
This the touch of my lips to yours, this the murmur
    of yearning.

This the far-off depth and height reflecting my own face,
This the thoughtful merge of myself, and the outlet again.

Do you guess I have some intricate purpose?
Well I have, for the Fourth-month showers have, and the
    mica on the side of a rock has.

Do you take it I would astonish?
Does the daylight astonish? does the early redstart
    twittering through the woods?
Do I astonish more than they?

This hour I tell things in confidence,
I might not tell everybody, but I will tell you.

From "Inscriptions," *Leaves of Grass*

By 1855, Whitman was finally ready to reveal the ecstatic utterings of his notebooks to the American public. Conventional publishers weren't interested in his unusual book, however, so he hired some friends to print it and actually set a number of pages himself. The first edition of *Leaves of Grass* was 95 pages long and contained 12 untitled poems. The frontispiece was an engraved photograph of the 36-year-old poet: a man with a short beard and jaunty hat who defied the formal conventions of the period by appearing in his shirtsleeves with his collar open, revealing the edge of his flannel undershirt.

Leaves of Grass was largely ignored, but among those who did read it, reaction was strong on both sides. A Boston paper attributed the book to an escaped lunatic. The poet John Greenleaf Whittier reportedly threw his copy into the fire. "One cannot leave it about for chance readers," said critic Charles Eliot Norton, "and would be sorry to know that any woman had looked into it past the title-page."

Others were moved and inspired by the book. "This man has brave stuff in him," one reviewer observed. Ralph Waldo Emerson, a well-respected poet and essayist, wrote Whitman a letter of highest praise. "I have great joy in it," he stated. "I greet you at the beginning of a great career, which yet must have had a long foreground somewhere, for such a start."

Although Whitman was to write two books of prose, he considered *Leaves of Grass* to be his life's work. He continually revised and expanded the book, publishing nine editions before his death in 1892.

The frontispiece for the first edition of Leaves of Grass

SONG OF MYSELF

From section 24

Walt Whitman, a kosmos, of Manhattan the son,
Turbulent, fleshy, sensual, eating, drinking and
     breeding,
No sentimentalist, no stander above men and
     women or apart from them,
No more modest than immodest.

Unscrew the locks from the doors!
Unscrew the doors themselves from their jambs!

Whoever degrades another degrades me,
And whatever is done or said returns at last to me.

Through me the afflatus surging and surging,
     through me the current and index.

I speak the pass-word primeval, I give the sign of
     democracy,
By God! I will accept nothing which all cannot have
     their counterpart of on the same terms.

Through me many long dumb voices,
Voices of the interminable generations of prison-
     ers and slaves,
Voices of the diseas'd and despairing and of thieves
     and dwarfs,
Voices of cycles of preparation and accretion,
And of the threads that connect the stars, and of
     wombs and of the father-stuff,
And of the rights of them the others are down
     upon,
Of the deform'd, trivial, flat, foolish, despised,
Fog in the air, beetles rolling balls of dung.

Through me forbidden voices,
Voices of sexes and lusts, voices veil'd and I
     remove the veil,
Voices indecent by me clarified and transfigur'd.

From "Inscriptions," *Leaves of Grass*

Toward midnight on April 12, 1861, Whitman was walking down Broadway after a night at the opera when he heard the sharp cries of newsboys hawking extra editions. The Confederates had opened fire on Fort Sumter in Charleston, South Carolina. It was the start of the Civil War.

At 42, the gray-bearded Whitman was too old to enlist, but his younger brother George did. In December 1862, following intense fighting at Fredericksburg, Virginia, Whitman saw his brother's misspelled name on a list of wounded and rushed to the camp hospitals to find him. George Whitman was only superficially injured and had already recovered by the time Whitman got to him, but Whitman remained in camp for more than a week, helping to care for the wounded. In his journal he wrote:

The results of the late battle are exhibited everywhere about here in thousands of cases, (hundreds die every day), in the camp, brigade, and division hospitals. These are merely tents, and sometimes very poor ones, the wounded lying on the ground, lucky if their blankets are spread on layers of pine or hemlock twigs, or small leaves. No cots; seldom even a mattress. It is pretty cold. The ground is frozen hard, and there is occasional snow. I go around from one case to another. I do not see that I do much good to these wounded and dying; but I cannot leave them. Once in a while some youngster holds on to me convulsively, and I do what I can for him; at any rate, stop with him and sit near him for hours, if he wishes it.

The bombardment of Fredericksburg

THE ARTILLERYMAN'S VISION

While my wife at my side lies slumbering, and
    the wars are over long,
And my head on the pillow rests at home, and the
    vacant midnight passes,
And through the stillness, through the dark, I hear,
    just hear, the breath of my infant,
There in the room as I wake from sleep this vision
    presses upon me;
The engagement opens there and then in fantasy
    unreal,
The skirmishers begin, they crawl cautiously ahead,
    I hear the irregular snap! snap!
I hear the sounds of the different missiles, the short
    t-h-t! t-h-t! of the rifle-balls,
I see the shells exploding leaving small white clouds,
    I hear the great shells shrieking as they pass,
The grape like the hum and whirr of wind through the
    trees, (tumultuous now the contest rages,)

All the scenes at the batteries rise in detail before
     me again,
The crashing and smoking, the pride of the men in
     their pieces,
The chief-gunner ranges and sights his piece and
     selects a fuse of the right time,
After firing I see him lean aside and look eagerly off
     to note the effect;
Elsewhere I hear the cry of a regiment charging, (the
     young colonel leads himself this time with
     brandish'd sword,)
I see the gaps cut by the enemy's volleys, (quickly
     fill'd up, no delay,)
I breathe the suffocating smoke, then the flat clouds
     hover low concealing all;
Now a strange lull for a few seconds, not a shot fired
     on either side,
Then resumed the chaos louder than ever, with eager
     calls and orders of officers,

(continued)

While from some distant part of the field
        the wind wafts to my ears a shout of
        applause, (some special success,)
And ever the sound of the cannon far or
        near, (rousing even in dreams a dev-
        ilish exultation and all the old mad
        joy in the depths of my soul,)
And ever the hastening of infantry shifting
        positions, batteries, cavalry, moving
hither and thither,

(The falling, dying, I heed not, the wounded
        dripping and red I heed not, some to
        the rear are hobbling,)
Grime, heat, rush, aides-de-camp galloping
        by or on a full run,
With the patter of small arms, the warning
        s-s-t of the rifles, (these in my vision
        I hear or see,)
And bombs bursting in air, and at night the
        varicolor'd rockets.

From "Drum-Taps," *Leaves of Grass*

The Civil War became for Whitman a personal mission of brotherhood and love. He moved to Washington, D.C., took a part-time job as a secretary in the army paymaster's office, and spent the rest of his time visiting soldiers. He dressed their wounds, read to them, and wrote letters home for those who weren't able to write. As he went about his wartime work, Whitman transformed his emotions and experiences into a collection of poems called "Drum-Taps."

On Good Friday, April 14, 1865, five days after General Robert E. Lee's surrender ended the Civil War, president Abraham Lincoln was shot in Washington; he died the next day. Whitman was visiting his mother in Brooklyn at the time, and it was with sorrow and disbelief that they read about the tragedy in the papers. "Mother prepared breakfast—and other meals afterward—as usual; but not a mouthful was eaten all day by either of us," Whitman wrote. "We each drank half a cup of coffee; that was all. Little was said. We got every newspaper morning and evening, and the frequent extras of that period, and pass'd them silently to each other." Whitman soon composed one of his best-known poems, "When Lilacs Last in the Dooryard Bloom'd," as a moving tribute to the slain leader.

Armory Square Hospital, Washington, D.C., where Whitman attended wounded soldiers

WHEN LILACS LAST IN THE DOORYARD BLOOM'D

Sections 1–6

1

When lilacs last in the dooryard bloom'd,
And the great star early droop'd in the western
 sky in the night,
I mourn'd, and yet shall mourn with ever-
 returning spring.

Ever-returning spring, trinity sure to me you
 bring,
Lilac blooming perennial and drooping star in
 the west,
And thought of him I love.

2

O powerful western fallen star!
O shades of night—O moody, tearful night!
O great star disappear'd—O the black murk that
 hides the star!
O cruel hands that hold me powerless—
 O helpless soul of me!
O harsh surrounding cloud that will not free
 my soul.

3

In the dooryard fronting an old farm-house near
 the white-wash'd palings,
Stands the lilac-bush tall-growing with heart-
 shaped leaves of rich green,
With many a pointed blossom rising delicate,
 with the perfume strong I love,
With every leaf a miracle—and from this bush in
 the dooryard,
With delicate-color'd blossoms and heart-shaped
 leaves of rich green,
A sprig with its flower I break.

4

In the swamp in secluded recesses,
A shy and hidden bird is warbling a song.

Solitary the thrush,
The hermit withdrawn to himself, avoiding the
 settlements,
Sings by himself a song.

Song of the bleeding throat,

Death's outlet song of life, (for well dear brother
    I know,

If thou wast not granted to sing thou would'st
    surely die.)

5

Over the breast of the spring, the land, amid
    cities,

Amid lanes and through old woods, where lately
    the violets peep'd from the ground,
    spotting the gray debris,

Amid the grass in the fields each side of the lanes,
    passing the endless grass,

Passing the yellow-spear'd wheat, every grain
    from its shroud in the dark-brown fields
    uprisen,

Passing the apple-tree blows of white and pink in
    the orchards,

Carrying a corpse to where it shall rest in the
    grave,

Night and day journeys a coffin.

6

Coffin that passes through lanes and streets,

Through day and night with the great cloud
    darkening the land,

With the pomp of the inloop'd flags with the cities
    draped in black,

With the show of the States themselves as of
    crape-veil'd women standing,

With processions long and winding and the
    flambeaus of the night,

With the countless torches lit, with the silent
    sea of faces and the unbared heads,

With the waiting depot, the arriving coffin,
    and the sombre faces,

With dirges through the night, with the thousand
    voices rising strong and solemn,

With all the mournful voices of the dirges pour'd
    around the coffin,

The dim-lit churches and the shuddering organs—
    where amid these you journey,

With the tolling tolling bells' perpetual clang,

Here, coffin that slowly passes,

I give you my sprig of lilac.

From "Memories of President Lincoln," *Leaves of Grass*

GOOD GRAY POET

For 10 years, Whitman made his home in Washington, D.C. He took a job as a clerk in the Department of the Interior, but his position came to an abrupt end when James Harlan was appointed as secretary. Dozens of government workers lost their jobs as Secretary Harlan reorganized the department for efficiency. Whitman's dismissal was different, however. Tipped off that Whitman had written a radical book of poetry, Secretary Harlan rifled through Whitman's desk and found a copy of *Leaves of Grass* in a drawer. A quick perusal confirmed his suspicion that the book was indecent. "I will not have the author of that book in this Department," he proclaimed.

By this time, Whitman was able to rely on a number of influential allies who took up his cause, and within 24 hours, he had a new job at the attorney general's office. The incident prompted fellow writer and friend William O'Connor to write a 46-page pamphlet championing Whitman as the poet of the American people. It was called *The Good Gray Poet*—a title by which Whitman is still known today.

Whitman pictured around 1870

TO A CERTAIN CIVILIAN

Did you ask dulcet rhymes from me?

Did you seek the civilian's peaceful and languishing
rhymes?

Did you find what I sang erewhile so hard to follow?

Why I was not singing erewhile for you to follow, to
understand—nor am I now;

(I have been born of the same as the war was born,

The drum-corps' rattle is ever to me sweet music, I love
well the martial dirge,

With slow wail and convulsive throb leading the officer's
funeral;)

What to such as you anyhow such a poet as I? therefore
leave my works,

And go lull yourself with what you can understand, and
with piano-tunes,

For I lull nobody, and you will never understand me.

From "Drum-Taps," *Leaves of Grass*

RECOVERY

On a January night in 1873, Whitman woke up in his fourth-floor Washington apartment to find himself partially paralyzed. A stroke had brought an end to the robust health of which he'd been so proud. That misfortune was soon followed by another: his mother died in May, an event Whitman called "the great dark cloud of my life."

Depressed and unable to work, Whitman moved in with his brother George's family in Camden, New Jersey. The two brothers quarreled often, the clash of the businessman and the poet. "I am very comfortable here indeed, but my *heart* is blank and lonesome utterly," Whitman confided to a friend.

Beginning in 1876, Whitman turned to another family for strength. The Staffords lived on a nearby farm; Whitman was a frequent and welcome guest. "Am with folks I love, & that love me," he noted after a visit. "Have had a real good old fashion'd time, first-rate for me—It is a farm, every thing plain & plenty, & blazing wood fires." During the summers, Whitman spent long hours outdoors, enjoying the meadows and woods. Gradually his health and spirits improved, and he later wrote about his recuperative experiences in *Specimen Days*.

The Lowland Brook *(1880), by Howard Pyle*

$\mathcal{S}$unday, Aug. 27 — Another day quite free from mark'd prostration and pain. It seems indeed as if peace and nutriment from heaven subtly filter into me as I slowly hobble down these country lanes and across fields, in the good air—as I sit here in solitude with Nature—open, voiceless, mystic, far removed, yet palpable, eloquent Nature…. Shall I tell you, reader, to what I attribute my already much-restored health? That I have been almost two years, off and on, without drugs and medicines, and daily in the open air. Last summer I found a particularly secluded little dell off one side by my creek, originally a large dug-out marl-pit, now abandon'd, fill'd with bushes, trees, grass, a group of willows, a straggling bank, and a spring of delicious water running right through the middle of it, with two or three little cascades. Here I retreated every hot day, and follow it up this summer. Here I realize the meaning of that old fellow who said he was seldom less alone than when alone. Never before did I get so close to Nature; never before did she come so close to me.

From *Specimen Days*

In 1884, at the age of 65, Whitman bought a small house in Camden, New Jersey. It was located near a railroad and a fertilizer factory, but Whitman didn't complain: the house on Mickle Street was his first real home, and it would be the last.

Surrounded by boxes, papers, and books, Whitman reviewed his many journals and edited his life—ripping out pages, crossing out words, changing initials to numbers. Certain things, he explained to a visitor, were "too sacred—too surely and only mine—to be perpetuated." For this reason, much about Whitman's life remains an enigma. He enhanced the mystery by claiming offhandedly to have fathered six children and by alluding to a love affair that ended in an "enforced separation." Conversely, it is clear to modern scholars that his deepest emotional attachments were to men, and he seems to have gone through periods of anxiety related to sexual ambiguity.

Whitman's friends made sure that he was not left alone in his old age. Some of them pitched in to buy him a buggy and a sorrel pony, and Whitman took great pleasure in his daily outings. In 1888, however, the jaunts came to an abrupt end when Whitman suffered another series of strokes. Too crippled to get around, Whitman hired a widow to care for him in exchange for her rent. His friend, a young man named Horace Traubel, ran errands for him and became his confidante, recording many conversations with him. Visitors came often to the little house on Mickle Street—literary intellectuals as well as the cab drivers and laborers whose company Whitman so enjoyed.

Camden, New Jersey: Walt Whitman's home

L. OF G.'S PURPORT

Not to exclude or demarcate, or pick out evils from
    their formidable masses (even to expose them,)
But add, fuse, complete, extend—and celebrate the immor-
    tal and the good.

Haughty this song, its words and scope,
To span vast realms of space and time,
Evolution—the cumulative—growths and generations.

Begun in ripen'd youth and steadily pursued,
Wandering, peering, dallying with all—war, peace, day and
    night absorbing,
Never even for one brief hour abandoning my task,
I end it here in sickness, poverty, and old age.

I sing of life, yet mind me well of death:
To-day shadowy Death dogs my steps, my seated shape, and
    has for years—
Draws sometimes close to me, as face to face.

From "Second Annex: Good-bye My Fancy," *Leaves of Grass*

DAYLIGHT FADING

Aware that little time was left him, Whitman undertook one of his last creative acts: he designed his own tomb and ordered its construction at Harleigh Cemetery in Camden. Set into a wooded hillside, the stately tomb was made of unpolished granite and closed with a graceful iron gate. As his health continued to decline, Whitman took comfort and pleasure in the thought of that peaceful resting place.

Walt Whitman died on March 26, 1892, at the age of 72. A friend's account read, "on the evening of Saturday, March 26th the daylight fading and a gentle rain falling outside the end came, simply and peacefully—Whitman conscious to the last, calm and undisturbed, his right hand resting in that of Horace Traubel."

Whitman's tomb at Harleigh Cemetery, Camden, New Jersey

OUT OF THE CRADLE ENDLESSLY ROCKING

Out of the cradle endlessly rocking,
Out of the mocking-bird's throat, the musical
shuttle,
Out of the Ninth-month midnight,
Over the sterile sands and the fields beyond, where
the child leaving his bed wander'd alone,
bareheaded, barefoot,
Down from the shower'd halo,
Up from the mystic play of shadows twining and
twisting as if they were alive,
Out from the patches of briers and blackberries,
From the memories of the bird that chanted to me,
From your memories sad brother, from the fitful
risings and fallings I heard,
From under that yellow half-moon late-risen and
swollen as if with tears,
From those beginning notes of yearning and love
there in the mist,

From the thousand responses of my heart never to
cease,
From the myriad thence-arous'd words,
From the word stronger and more delicious than any,

From such as now they start the scene revisiting,
As a flock, twittering, rising, or overhead passing,
Borne hither, ere all eludes me, hurriedly,
A man, yet by these tears a little boy again,
Throwing myself on the sand, confronting the waves,
I, chanter of pains and joys, uniter of here and
hereafter,
Taking all hints to use them, but swiftly leaping
beyond them,
A reminiscence sing.

Once Paumanok,
When the lilac-scent was in the air and Fifth-month
grass was growing,

(continued)

Up this seashore in some briers,

Two feather'd guests from Alabama, two together,

And their nest, and four light-green eggs spotted
      with brown,

And every day the he-bird to and fro near at hand,

And every day the she-bird crouch'd on her nest,
      silent, with bright eyes

And every day I, a curious boy, never too close,
      never disturbing them,

Cautiously peering, absorbing, translating.

Shine! shine! shine!

Pour down your warmth, great sun!

While we bask, we two together.

Two together!

Winds blow south, or winds blow north,

Day come white, or night come black,

Home, or rivers and mountains from home,

Singing all time, minding no time,

While we two keep together.

Till of a sudden,

May-be kill'd, unknown to her mate,

One forenoon the she-bird crouch'd not on
      the nest,

Nor return'd that afternoon, nor the next,

Nor ever appear'd again.

And thenceforward all summer in the sound
      of the sea,

And at night under the full of the moon in calmer
      weather,

Over the hoarse surging of the sea,

Or flitting from brier to brier by day,

I saw, I heard at intervals the remaining one, the
      he-bird,

The solitary guest from Alabama.

Blow! blow! blow!

Blow up sea-winds along Paumanok's shore;

I wait and I wait till you blow my mate to me.

Yes, when the stars glisten'd,

All night long on the prong of a moss scallop'd stake,
Down almost amid the slapping waves,
Sat the lone singer wonderful causing tears.

He call'ed on his mate,
He pour'd forth the meaning which I of all men
      know.
Yes my brother I know,
The rest might not, but I have treasur'd every note,
For more than once dimly down to the beach
      gliding,
Silent, avoiding the moonbeams, blending myself
      with the shadows,
Recalling now the obscure shapes, the echoes, the
      sounds and sights after their sorts,
The white arms out in the breakers tirelessly
      tossing,
I, with bare feet, a child, the wind wafting my hair,
Listen'd long and long.

Listen'd to keep, to sing, now translating the notes,
Following you my brother.

Soothe! soothe! soothe!
Close on its wave soothes the wave behind,
And again another behind embracing and lapping,
      every one close,
But my love soothes not me, not me.

Low hangs the moon, it rose late,
It is lagging—O I think it is heavy with love, with love.

O madly the sea pushes upon the land,
With love, with love.

O night! do I not see my love fluttering out among the
      breakers?
What is that little black thing I see there in the white?

Loud! loud! loud!
Loud I call to you, my love!

High and clear I shoot my voice over the waves,
Surely you must know who is here, is here,
You must know who I am, my love.

(continued)

Low-hanging moon!
What is that dusky spot in your brown yellow?
O it is the shape, the shape of my mate!
O Moon do not keep her from me any longer.

Land! land! O land!
Whichever way I turn, O I think you could give
me my mate back again if you only would,
For I am almost sure I see her dimly whichever
way I look.

O rising stars!
Perhaps the one I want so much will rise,
will rise with some of you.

O throat! O trembling throat!
Sound clearer through the atmosphere!
Pierce the woods, the earth,
Somewhere listening to catch you must be the
one I want.

Shake out carols!

Solitary here, the night's carols!

Carols of lonesome love! death's carols!
Carols under that lagging, yellow, waning moon!
O under that moon where she droops almost down
into the sea!
O reckless despairing carols.

But soft! sink low!
Soft! let me just murmur,
And do you wait a moment you husky-nois'd sea,
For somewhere I believe I heard my mate responding
to me,
So faint, I must be still, be still to listen,
But not altogether still, for then she might not come
immediately to me.

Hither my love!
Here I am! here!
With this just-sustain'd note I announce myself
to you,

This gentle call is for you my love, for you.

Do not be decoy'd elsewhere,

That is the whistle of the wind, it is not my voice,

That is the fluttering, the fluttering of the spray,

Those are the shadows of leaves.

O darkness! O in vain!

O I am very sick and sorrowful.

O brown halo in the sky near the moon, drooping upon
　　　the sea!

O troubled reflection in the sea!

O throat! O throbbing heart!

And I singing uselessly, uselessly all the night.

O past! O happy life! O songs of joy!

In the air, in the woods, over fields,

Loved! loved! loved! loved! loved!

But my mate no more, no more with me!

We two together no more.

The aria sinking,

All else continuing, the stars shining,

The winds blowing, the notes of the bird
　　　continuous echoing,

With angry moans the fierce old mother
　　　incessantly moaning,

On the sands of Paumanok's shore gray and
　　　rustling,

The yellow half-moon enlarged, sagging down,
　　　drooping, the face of the sea almost
　　　touching,

The boy ecstatic, with his bare feet the waves, with
　　　his hair the atmosphere dallying,

The love in the heart long pent, now loose, now at
　　　last tumultuously bursting,

The aria's meaning, the ears, the soul, swiftly
　　　depositing,

The strange tears down the cheeks coursing,

The colloquy there, the trio, each uttering,

(continued)

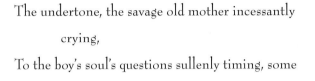

The undertone, the savage old mother incessantly
    crying,
To the boy's soul's questions sullenly timing, some
    drown'd secret hissing,
To the outsetting bard.

Demon or bird! (said the boy's soul,)
Is it indeed toward your mate you sing? or is it
    really to me?
For I, that was a child, my tongue's use sleeping,
    now I have heard you,
Now in a moment I know what I am for, I awake,
And already a thousand singers, a thousand songs,
    clearer, louder and more sorrowful than
    yours,
A thousand warbling echoes have started to life
    within me, never to die.

O you singer solitary, singing by yourself,
    projecting me,

O solitary me listening, never more shall I cease
    perpetuating you,

Never more shall I escape, never more the
    reverberations,
Never more the cries of unsatisfied love be absent
    from me,
Never again leave me to be the peaceful child I was
    before what there in the night,
By the sea under the yellow and sagging moon,
The messenger there arous'd, the fire, the sweet
    hell within,
The unknown want, the destiny of me.

O give me the clew! (it lurks in the night here
    somewhere,)
O if I am to have so much, let me have more!

A word then, (for I will conquer it,)
The word final, superior to all,
Subtle, sent up—what is it?—I listen;

Are you whispering it, and have been all the time,
you sea-waves?
Is that it from your liquid rims and wet sands?

Whereto answering, the sea,
Delaying not, hurrying not,
Whisper'd me through the night, and very plainly
before daybreak,
Lisp'd to me the low and delicious word death,
And again death, death, death, death,
Hissing melodious, neither like the bird nor like
my arous'd child's heart,
But edging near as privately for me rustling at my
feet,
Creeping thence steadily up to my ears and laving
me softly all over,
Death, death, death, death, death.

Which I do not forget,
But fuse the song of my dusky demon and brother,

That he sang to me in the moonlight on
Paumanok's gray beach,
With the thousand responsive songs at random,
My own songs awaked from that hour,
And with them the key, the word up from the
waves,
The word of the sweetest song and all songs,
That strong and delicious word which, creeping to
my feet,
(Or like some old crone rocking the cradle,
swathed in sweet garments, bending aside,)
The sea whisper'd me.

From "Sea-Drift," *Leaves of Grass*

45

ACKNOWLEDGMENTS

PHOTO CREDITS

Alamy (Archive Images, Niday Picture Library); The Bettmann Archive; Culver Pictures, Inc.; The Granger Collection; Library of Congress Prints & Photographs Division [LC-USZ62-79942]; North Wind Picture Archives; Stock Montage; The Walt Whitman Archive [yal.00012]; *Winter scene in Brooklyn, New York 1817–20*, by Francis Guy. Oil painting on canvas 4' x 8'1," Museum of the City of New York #53.2

SELECTED WORKS BY WALT WHITMAN

Since the first edition appeared in 1855, Leaves of Grass *has never been out of print. Whitman revised and expanded the book until his death; the contents listed below are for the final edition of 1892.*

Leaves of Grass
Subdivisions:
Inscriptions
Children of Adam
Calamus
Birds of Passage
Sea-Drift
By the Roadside

Drum-Taps
Memories of President Lincoln
Autumn Rivulets
Whispers of Heavenly Death
From Noon to Starry Night
Songs of Parting
First Annex: Sands at Seventy
Second Annex: Good-bye My Fancy

PROSE
Democratic Vistas, 1871
Specimen Days, 1882

Poems and extracts appearing in this work:

"The Artilleryman's Vision" 26–28

Democratic Vistas 19

"L. of G.'s Purport" 37

Leaves of Grass preface 17

"One's-Self I Sing" 15

"Out of the Cradle Endlessly Rocking" 39–45

"Song of Myself" (from Section 24) 23

"Song of Myself" (Section 1) 7

"Song of Myself" (Section 19) 21

Specimen Days 35

"There Was a Child Went Forth" 9–11

"To a Certain Civilian" 33

"When I Heard the Learn'd Astronomer" 13

"When I Read the Book" 1

"When Lilacs Last in the Dooryard Bloom'd" (Sections 1–6) 30–31

American Civil War 24, 29

Aurora (newspaper) 16

Brooklyn, New York 8, 12, 29

Camden, New Jersey 34, 36, 38

Democratic Party 18

"Drum-Taps" 29

Emerson, Ralph Waldo 5, 22

Franklin Evans 18

Free Soil Democrats 18

Great Fire of New York (1835) 14

Harlan, James 32

Harleigh Cemetery (N.J.) 38

Kaplan, Justin 20

Leaves of Grass 5, 6, 22, 32

Lee, Robert E. 29

Lincoln, Abraham 29

Long Island, New York 8, 14

Long Islander (newspaper) 16

New York, New York 18, 20, 24

New York Mirror (newspaper) 12

Norton, Charles Eliot 22

O'Connor, William 32

   The Good Gray Poet 32

Specimen Days 34

Stafford family 34

Traubel, Horace 36, 38

Washington, D.C. 29, 32, 34

"When Lilacs Last in the Dooryard Bloom'd" 29

Whitman, George (brother) 24, 34

Whitman, Louisa (mother) 8, 29, 34

Whitman, Walt
   childhood 8
   critical reception 5, 6, 22
   cultural interests 18, 24
   death 22, 38
   education 5, 12
   first job 12
   government jobs 29, 32
   illness 34, 36, 38
   later years 36, 38
   newspaper work 16, 18, 20
   personal relationships 36
   physical appearance 18, 20, 22
   poetic style 5, 6
   poetic themes 5
   political views 18
   printing apprenticeship 12
   publications 18, 22, 29
   schoolteacher 14, 20
   siblings 8, 20, 24, 34
   tomb 38
   views on slavery 18
   wartime volunteer 24, 29

Whitman, Walter (father) 8, 14, 20

Whittier, John Greenleaf 22

Published by Creative Education
P.O. Box 227, Mankato, Minnesota 56002
Creative Education is an imprint of The Creative Company
www.thecreativecompany.us
Design by Stephanie Blumenthal
Production by The Design Lab
Illustrations by Rob Day
Art direction by Rita Marshall
Printed in the United States of America

Library of Congress Cataloging-in-Publication Data
Loewen, Nancy.
Walt Whitman / by Nancy Loewen.
p. cm. — (Voices in Poetry)
Includes index.
Summary: An exploration of the life and work of 19th-century
American writer Walt Whitman, whose poetry is known for
both its passionate celebration of American life and its direct,
speechlike style.
ISBN 978-1-60818-329-6
1. Whitman, Walt, 1819–1892—Juvenile literature. 2. Poets,
American—19th century—Biography—Juvenile literature. 3.
Young adult poetry, American. I. Title.
PS3232.L63 2014
811'.3—dc23   [B]   2013030158

CCSS: RL.4.1, 2, 3, 4, 5, 6; RL.5.2, 4, 6, 7; RI.5.1, 2, 3, 8
First Edition
9 8 7 6 5 4 3 2 1